SEEK

Julia A. Royston

BK
ROYSTON
Publishing

I0192079

BK Royston Publishing
Jeffersonville, IN 47131
http://www.bkroystonpublishing.com
bkroystonpublishing@gmail.com

© Copyright – 2025

All Rights Reserved. No part of this book may be
reproduced, stored in a retrieval system, or
transmitted by any means without the written
permission of the author.

Cover Design: BK Royston Publishing
Cover Photo: Jonathan Snorten

ISBN-13: 978-1-967282-20-3

King James Version Scriptural Text – Public Domain

Printed in the United States of America

Dedication

Dreams are great.

Visions are wonderful.

Plans are even better.

With the plans in your hand, it's time to Seek the solution to your problem, answer to your question and pathway to success.

You'll get there when you Seek.

———

Theme Scripture

Ask, and it shall be given you; **Seek**, and ye shall find; knock, and it shall be opened unto you:

Matthew 7:7 (KJV)

Acknowledgements

I thank my Lord and Savior Jesus Christ for giving me another opportunity to introduce more people to you. I thank you for entrusting this gift to me. Lord, let your Spirit move, guide and empower through this book to the people who will read it.

To my husband, Brian K. Royston, the love of my life, for loving and cheering me on so much that I can be and do all that God has placed in me. I love you.

To my mom, my greatest supporter and best friend. To my dad, who is in Heaven, who I know is proud of me and always encouraged me to go for it. Thanks to all the rest of my family for their love and support.

A special thank you to Rev. and Mrs. Claude R. Royston for their love and support.

To the rest of my clients, friends and family, thank you and love you always.

Let's go!

Table of Contents

Dedication   iii

Theme Scripture   iv

Acknowledgements   v

Introduction   ix

WHAT ARE YOU SEEKING FOR?   1

SEEK YOUR BROTHERS   5

DON'T SEEK YOUR OWN HEART   9

SEEK HIM WITH ALL OF YOUR HEART AND SOUL   13

SEEKING PEACE IN THE WRONG PLACE   17

SEEK REST   21

SEEK SAFETY   25

SEEK THE RIGHT WAY   29

SEEK AND COMMIT YOUR CAUSE 33

SEEK IN THE MORNING 37

SEEK TO HELP THE POOR 41

WILL NOT FORSAKE THE SEEKER 45

SEEK THY FACE 49

ONE THING TO SEEK AFTER 53

SEEK THE LORD AND NOT WANT 57

SEEK PEACE AND PURSUE IT 61

SEEK EARLY 65

SEEK AND LIVE 69

SHAMED TO SEEK GOD 73

THE SELFISH SEEKER 77

SEEK FIRST THE KINGDOM 81

About the Author 85

More Books By This Author 86

Introduction

This is Part 2 of the scripture Matthew 7:7 and the second devotional in this particular series. It's time to Seek. This part is hard for people because some people need the whole plan, all of the money, the first step in the dream, the middle and the end of the dream up front as well as all of the people who are going to help bring the vision to pass.

Sorry to tell you, but it doesn't work like that. In the Bible, some were healed as they went. One man had to dip seven times to get healed and didn't get healed until the seventh time.

Abraham was told to leave everything that he knew, take your whole family, his empire, just start walking and God would show him where to go only after he started walking. I wonder how that trip went with the family and all of the property, oxen and extended family that came along.

We must first always Seek God's heart, will, plan and direction for our lives, trusting only in Him and the next steps, but we don't always get the whole plan.

You ready? You've asked. Now it's time to get your shoes on, pack up and Seek.

Let's go!

WHAT ARE YOU SEEKING FOR?

"And a certain man found him, and behold, he was wandering in the field: and the man asked him, saying, What **seek**est thou?"

Genesis 37:15 (KJV)

At the age and stage that I am in right now, I often ask myself when going from one room to the next, what did I come in here to look for? It happens, just keep living. All jokes aside, you can't truly seek for something with the full intention of finding it unless you know what you are seeking for. What is it? What are you after? How will you know it when you find it or stumble across it or someone brings it to you? If you don't know, you will accept anything. You will take anything if you don't know what exactly you are looking for. Whether it be a mate, a job, a house, a car or a life, know what you want before you start moving, searching and asking because someone will offer you anything, and only you can decide whether it is what you are wanting, seeking and desiring or not.

So, I ask you, what are you seeking for? Take some time. Pray about it. Ask God for guidance. Write it down. Compare what you wrote with what you see and offered. If it doesn't match, say no.

REFLECTION

_____

_____

_____

_____

_____

_____

_____

_____

_____

_____

_____

_____

_____

_____

_____

_____

_____

_____

_____

_____

_____

_____

REFLECTION

_____

_____

_____

_____

_____

_____

_____

_____

_____

_____

_____

_____

_____

_____

_____

_____

_____

_____

_____

_____

_____

_____

_____

_____

SEEK YOUR BROTHERS

"And he said, I **seek** my brethren: tell me, I pray thee, where they feed their flocks."

Genesis 37:16 (KJV)

We've all heard the term find the people who are kin to you and not necessarily who is *skin* to you. Meaning, brothers or sisters may not have come from your same mother and father but they are a true brother or sister indeed. In my lifetime, I've found people whom God has placed in my life for seasons that I needed a brother or sister close to me. I have two wonderful sisters who will roll out if anything goes on, but they may not be in my same space or place to help. But God always has somebody.

In this instance, the people needed help and wanted to feed their flocks without worry about anything happening to them, fear of being stolen or harmed in any way. The man said, "Go find my brethren, my kinfolk, my people, my company, my business people, my church or my non-profit folks and they will treat you right."

"Who is my mother or my father?" Jesus asked. He answered that His real family is those who do God's will.

Where are your kinfolks? Where are your real brothers and sisters? Seek them and get the help that you need.

REFLECTION

_____

REFLECTION

_____

_____
_____
_____
_____
_____
_____
_____
_____
_____
_____
_____
_____
_____
_____
_____
_____
_____
_____
_____
_____
_____
_____
_____
_____
_____
_____
_____
_____
_____
_____

DON'T SEEK YOUR OWN HEART

"And it shall be unto you for a fringe, that ye may look upon it, and remember all the commandments of the Lord, and do them ; and that ye **seek** not after your own heart and your own eyes."

Numbers 15:39 (KJV)

I have asked my husband many times, "Are you looking at the same thing I'm looking at?" He will say, "Yes" but I will still ask him again, "What do you see?" Sometimes he is looking at the same thing that I am looking at and sees something totally different. Why? Perspective. Point of Reference and sometimes it's your past. You bring all parts of you into your perspective, eyesight and insight. So sometimes you can't trust your own heart and your own eyes. It doesn't always tell or show the truth of the situation, people and purpose of the actions. We often use the scripture about God said that man was not good to be alone just for marriage, but it is not good for any of us to totally be alone. Why? We may miss something we've been seeking, begging, pleading, preparing and planning for because we don't see the answer right in front of us. You were looking at the wrong thing but your answer was there and you missed it. You had a bad experience once that looked like what you're looking at but you judge the new thing based on the old thing.

Don't seek with your own heart but with the heart and eyes of God. God, open up our eyes so that we can see like You see and not as we see.

REFLECTION

_____

REFLECTION

SEEK HIM WITH ALL OF YOUR HEART AND SOUL

"But if from thence thou shalt **seek** the Lord thy God, thou shalt find him, if thou **seek** him with all thy heart and with all thy soul."

Deuteronomy 4:29 (KJV)

You can tell when people are not all in. They have excuses, reasons why not, and their language is filled with doubt. The idea, project, job, business and/or relationship is doomed from the start because you're not all in. You have not committed with your entire self. Only half of your heart, only half of your energy and only half of your results will be realized because you're not all in. Even having a full-time job and a part-time hustle will never get the full you because you're torn between the full-time job and the part-time hustle; everything is shared. But what if you were able to give your full self to one? I encourage you to give your full self to THE ONE. The ONE AND ONLY God, the Father, Jehovah, King of Kings and Lord of Lords. Seek Him with all of yourself. Let your heart, soul and mind be all in to His will, His way and His plan for your life. Don't leave anything out. Don't keep anything back, but seek Him with all of it, everything, for eternity.

Remember, your heart and soul are the most important parts of you given to the only important one of all time, GOD Himself.

REFLECTION

_____

REFLECTION

_____
_____
_____
_____
_____
_____
_____
_____
_____
_____
_____
_____
_____
_____
_____
_____
_____
_____
_____
_____
_____
_____
_____
_____
_____
_____

SEEKING PEACE IN THE WRONG PLACE

"Thou shalt not **seek** their peace nor their prosperity all thy days forever."

Deuteronomy 23:6 (KJV)

All money is not good money and all peace is not true peace when you seek it in the wrong place with the wrong people. Because we live in a society that wants immediate gratification, we sometimes align ourselves with people, get the wrong advice and make decisions that are NOT in our best interest. These irrational or incorrect decisions can have long-lasting impact on our current lives, the future and the next generation.

In this scripture, because of disobedience and evil, God said, "You won't be able to find or seek peace or have prosperity, all of your days forever." What a judgment! What a harsh word! But God knows everything about us. God is gracious, but when we are set on doing things our way, just like any great Father, we have to suffer the consequences. It is best to seek Him first and then, no matter the situation, all of it will work for our good. It may not feel good or look good, but in the end, it will work for our good.

If there is trouble going on in your life, seek God's perfect peace and He will give it if we keep our minds on Him.

REFLECTION

REFLECTION

_____
_____
_____
_____
_____
_____
_____
_____
_____
_____
_____
_____
_____
_____
_____
_____
_____
_____
_____
_____
_____
_____
_____
_____
_____
_____
_____

SEEK REST

"Then Naomi, her mother-in-law, said unto her, My daughter, shall I not **seek** rest for thee, that it may be well with thee?"

Ruth 3:1 (KJV)

I have a hard time with rest. I'm good with work, but rest is something that is a struggle for me. I have to make a conscious effort to get rest. Now, I am striving to listen to my body more and not let it MAKE me rest, but it takes me a minute to get to the actual process of resting state.

Naomi and her daughter-in-law Ruth had been in an unsettling upheaval and grievous place. Ruth lost her husband and Naomi lost her son. A woman uncovered with no male figure in ancient times had no rest. There was a constant struggle for provision, a voice and justice. Women were considered property or responsibility of someone. Whether it was their husband, uncle or son, but he had to be male and related. But with the death of not one, but both of Naomi's sons and her husband, they were alone and the responsibility of no one. They must survive on their own. They must find shelter, food, pay taxes, worship and protect themselves. Naomi said, "We came down here in this strange land for protection, but now we have no protection. I must seek rest, covering, protection for you and me, and the best place for that is home, Bethlehem."

That was Naomi's promise to Ruth for following her back to Bethlehem, to seek rest for herself and her daughter-in-law. Do you work best in chaos or rest? The bible says, 'Seek rest.'

REFLECTION

_____
_____
_____
_____
_____
_____
_____
_____
_____
_____
_____
_____
_____
_____
_____
_____
_____
_____
_____
_____
_____
_____
_____
_____
_____
_____
_____

REFLECTION

_____
_____
_____
_____
_____
_____
_____
_____
_____
_____
_____
_____
_____
_____
_____
_____
_____
_____
_____
_____
_____
_____
_____
_____
_____
_____

SEEK SAFETY

"Abide thou with me, fear not: for he that **seek**eth my life **seek**eth thy life: but with me thou shalt be in safeguard."

1 Samuel 22:23 (KJV)

Safety first. That's what my parents always told us. Whatever you do, don't put yourself in harm's way. Stick together. Do you have a quarter for the pay phone? Yes, I'm pay phone old. We came together and we are leaving together. I don't care how cute he is and his car, you are riding back in the old 'got us here safe and will get us back home safe' car.

You are safest when you stick together. Wandering off by yourself can easily get you attacked and if you're alone, you can't get away as easily or think of the best way to escape. Seek safety. Away from life's storms. Away from predators who seek to not only do you harm but destroy your life.

You think that you are young, strong, smart and can think quickly on your feet, but the enemy today is more wicked than ever. Don't play on the devil's territory, young or old. He's playing for keeps and eternity is the sentence.

God's way is the safe way and the best way.
Seek safety.

REFLECTION

REFLECTION

_____

_____
_____
_____
_____
_____
_____
_____
_____
_____
_____
_____
_____
_____
_____
_____
_____
_____
_____
_____
_____
_____
_____
_____
_____

SEEK THE RIGHT WAY

"Then I proclaimed a fast there, at the river of Ahava, that we might afflict ourselves before our God, to **seek** of him a right way."

Ezra 8:21 (KJV)

I have written this many times and will say it again. I don't like getting lost. My father-in-law says that's about control, I resemble that remark, but more importantly, I don't like getting lost. I don't like wasting time wandering around with no clear-cut direction to get to the said destination. I know where we are trying to go, but getting there is still up for grabs.

So, in Ezra 8, he proclaimed a fast, stopped eating or drinking, to seek God's face to Him the right way. We don't have time to go the wrong way, wasting time going our own way but want to only go the way God wants us to go in the correct, right and divine direction for our business, career and life. Furthermore, on a fast, you are hungry in your stomach but your ears should be on high alert. The purpose of a fast is to petition His heart and hand for direction, hear and listen for direction or instruction and then move quickly and execute in excellence what He said.

Fasting may help you lose weight, which is all well and good, but if I have a problem, I am fasting to get an answer. There should be a point to my fast, mix the fast with faith, have an inclined ear to hear what God is saying, get up close to God's mouth, so I don't miss anything, and then do what He says.

So, in your seeking, Seek the Right Way.

REFLECTION

_____
_____
_____
_____
_____
_____
_____
_____
_____
_____
_____
_____
_____
_____
_____
_____
_____
_____
_____
_____
_____
_____
_____
_____
_____
_____
_____
_____
_____

REFLECTION

_____

_____
_____
_____
_____
_____
_____
_____
_____
_____
_____
_____
_____
_____
_____
_____
_____
_____
_____
_____
_____
_____
_____
_____
_____
_____
_____
_____

SEEK AND COMMIT YOUR CAUSE

"I would **seek** unto God, and unto God would I commit my cause."

Job 5:8 (KJV)

What is the cause that can lead to an effect or an effort? Sometimes we have a cause, reason, problem or situation, but it is not worth the effort to take to God. Even though we should ask Him and Seek Him about everything, some things we don't think are worth it or have a high enough value to commit to or put an effort to.

Not only are the big things worth seeking God about, but everything is worth seeking God about. Leave it in His hands. Take your hands off of it. Remove yourself, leave it at the altar, tell God you've done and watch Him work it out.

The first act, of course, is the seeking. But the next major act is the commitment into His hands. Most people are okay with the seeking part but never take their hands off of it. They are always striving, trying, working on and doing things to figure it out on their own. Only to make a bigger mess, cause long-term harm, lose the investment of time and resources along with the energy, effort and time wasted. God can and will recover all, but it could have been sooner and without so much drama if we had just committed the cause to Him.

Seek Him and commit.

REFLECTION

_____

_____
_____
_____
_____
_____
_____
_____
_____
_____
_____
_____
_____
_____
_____
_____
_____
_____
_____
_____
_____
_____
_____
_____
_____
_____
_____
_____

REFLECTION

_____

_____

_____

_____

_____

_____

_____

_____

_____

_____

_____

_____

_____

_____

_____

_____

_____

_____

_____

_____

_____

_____

SEEK IN THE MORNING

"… and thou shalt **seek** me in the morning,"

Job 7:21 (KJV)

Don't reach out to me late at night unless it is a family emergency. I am not good after 7:00 p.m. Once I start taking my earrings out of my ears, it is a wrap. I am done. I am ready for bed. If I could lie down by 6:00 p.m., I would be even better. Why? I do my best work in the morning. By lunchtime, I probably have worked up to 6 hours. One day, I will really stop working around 2:00 p.m. but that's another book.

In the morning, my house is quiet. My thoughts are fresh. God might have awakened me around 3:00 a.m. and I have been thinking about what to write or what to do for 2 hours before I really get out of bed. I know that this is not everyone's testimony but I work best in the morning.

God never sleeps nor slumbers. He is listening and ready to answer our call any time of the night or day, but when you seek Him in the morning, you are offering up the first fruits of your day to Him. You are asking Him to cover you, show you and show up for you as well as you are seeking His direction for the day and week.

Seek Him in the morning. Don't wait until everything has fallen apart by lunch and you're exhausted, disgusted and ready to quit by the evening. I guarantee you that if you talk to Him, He'll prepare you for your day, give you the inside scoop, and the enemy will not know what hit him. Seek God in the morning.

REFLECTION

_____
_____
_____
_____
_____
_____
_____
_____
_____
_____
_____
_____
_____
_____
_____
_____
_____
_____
_____
_____
_____
_____
_____
_____
_____
_____
_____

REFLECTION

_____
_____
_____
_____
_____
_____
_____
_____
_____
_____
_____
_____
_____
_____
_____
_____
_____
_____
_____
_____
_____
_____
_____
_____
_____

SEEK TO HELP THE POOR

―――――

"His children shall **seek** to please the poor, and his hands shall restore their goods."

Job 20:10 (KJV)

"For I was an hungred, and ye gave me meat: I was thirsty, and ye gave me drink: I was a stranger, and ye took me in:… In as much as ye have done it unto one of the least of these my brethren, ye have done it unto me." (Matthew 25:35, 40 KJV) Those are the words of Jesus. He also said, "For ye have **the poor** always with you…" (Matthew 26:11 KJV)

Helping the poor is a part of our Christian duty. Some people have had circumstances beyond their control that contributes to their poverty. Others have made poor decisions which have resulted in poverty. The children, the elderly and those disabled are the most vulnerable among us and need the most help.

What can you do to help the poor? What can you contribute out of the multitude of your substance to help someone in need? Do you have just enough or more than enough? Do you turn a blind eye to those who are in need or do you seek to help those who may be poor, less fortunate or just need some direction or support in a time of need. We normally think of poor or poverty as just food, clothing, shelter or money, but some people have a poor outlook, poor work habits or work ethic and others see themselves in a poor light. They may have all of the material things they need and can spare some for others but have a poverty mentality and spirit.

In our seeking, seek to help the poor because the poor ye will have with you always.

REFLECTION

_____

REFLECTION

_____
_____
_____
_____
_____
_____
_____
_____
_____
_____
_____
_____
_____
_____
_____
_____
_____
_____
_____
_____
_____
_____
_____
_____
_____

WILL NOT FORSAKE THE SEEKER

"And they that know thy name will put their trust in thee: for thou, Lord, hast not forsaken them that **seek** thee."

Psalm 9:10 (KJV)

No matter what is going on or no matter what it looks like, He won't leave you. Others will come and then circle back to you again. But God is not leaving you. He is trustworthy. He is loyal. He is faithful. He is sovereign. He asks no one if He can associate with you, bless you, be with you, stay with you or love you. He stands alone. So, if He says, He's not leaving, He means it. You can take it to the bank. He especially is not leaving those who trust Him and seek Him.

When you trust God, there are things that you do, places you go and things you say that prove that you trust Him. Despite what others do or say or what the truth of what you see is saying, trust God and then seek Him for your next move. Seek Him for what you should or should not be doing, saying or believing. Seek

Him about your next steps, what is coming next, who can be trusted, where you should spend your time and your money.

The perfect plan and actions for your life are when you trust and seek God. Everything will come and fall into place. You may get disappointed that things didn't turn out like you wanted, but remember, those who diligently seek Him will be blessed and fulfill their purpose.

He ain't leaving you.

REFLECTION

_____

_____
_____
_____
_____
_____
_____
_____
_____
_____
_____
_____
_____
_____
_____
_____
_____
_____
_____
_____
_____
_____
_____
_____
_____

REFLECTION

_____
_____
_____
_____
_____
_____
_____
_____
_____
_____
_____
_____
_____
_____
_____
_____
_____
_____
_____
_____
_____
_____
_____
_____
_____
_____

SEEK THY FACE

"This is the generation of them that **seek** him, that **seek** thy face, O Jacob. Selah."

Psalm 24:6 (KJV)

Have you ever had your mother or father say, "Look at me." They wanted you to look them in the eyes when they were talking to you and when you responded. Holding your head down meant that you were thinking, hiding or lying and probably all three. There is something about looking someone in the face and telling a lie that meant that you were good at lying. You were probably going to tell more lies and when the truth was found out, "You told me a bold face lie." A lie is a lie, but there's something about telling a lie face to face that somehow makes it worse. A lie on paper, in a text message or via email is still a lie but when you tell one to my face, it takes everything to a whole new level.

Psalms 24 says to not only seek God but you want to seek His face. Now we know that no man has seen God face to face and lived, but when you seek God's face, you are up close. You are focused on Him and Him alone. No distractions, no other people, places, things, motives, agendas or alternatives, just God.

I have a problem. I need an answer. I am confused. I need direction. I got myself into a mess and I have to get out. I did the wrong thing. I caused something terrible to happen and I not only need to ask God and repent but I need to get up close in His face to get the answer.

This is the generation that not only is going to seek God, but needs to seek God's face.

REFLECTION

_____

_____
_____
_____
_____
_____
_____
_____
_____
_____
_____
_____
_____
_____
_____
_____
_____
_____
_____
_____
_____
_____
_____
_____
_____

REFLECTION

_____

_____
_____
_____
_____
_____
_____
_____
_____
_____
_____
_____
_____
_____
_____
_____
_____
_____
_____
_____
_____
_____
_____
_____
_____
_____
_____

ONE THING TO SEEK AFTER

"One thing have I desired of the Lord, that will I **seek** after; that I may dwell in the house of the Lord all the days of my life, to behold the beauty of the Lord, and to enquire in his temple."

Psalm 27:4 (KJV)

I have asked coaching clients that if money was no object and someone paid their bills for 1 year, what would they love to do with their time? The majority of those I ask cannot tell me. Some people don't have dreams, goals and ambitions beyond where they are right now. The first 20 years of working, I worked to have money to pay bills, buy clothes and travel. The last 20 years of working, I worked to be able to do whatever I wanted and loved to do. I worked the hardest to plan, prepare, pray and pursue my dream. I kept my eyes on the prize. No matter how the students behaved, the teachers misbehaved or the administrators did nothing to help, I kept going. I knew that my current situation was not permanent and although I didn't know everything that was going to happen, I knew that that was something better than the current situation.

Like David, the first thing is that you have to know is what you desire. Once you know that, then it's time to seek after it with everything that you have within in you. It won't be easy, perfect or without work but seek after it and you may be pleasantly surprised at what God blesses you with AFTER you Seek.

What is the one thing that you desire?

REFLECTION

_____

_____
_____
_____
_____
_____
_____
_____
_____
_____
_____
_____
_____
_____
_____
_____
_____
_____
_____
_____
_____
_____
_____
_____
_____
_____
_____

REFLECTION

_____

_____

_____

_____

_____

_____

_____

_____

_____

_____

_____

_____

_____

_____

_____

_____

_____

_____

_____

_____

_____

_____

_____

_____

_____

_____

_____

SEEK THE LORD AND NOT WANT

"The young lions do lack, and suffer hunger: but they that **seek** the Lord shall not want any good thing."

Psalm 34:10 (KJV)

The most famous Psalm to me is Psalm 23—the Lord is my shepherd and I shall not want—but this scripture struck me even harder because sheep must have a shepherd at all times. They are creatures that are often led astray, preyed upon by other creatures and can easily lose focus and come to their demise.

But in Psalm 34:10, we find out that the young lions do sometimes lack, which is odd because we always think of lions as predators, hunters and the king of the jungle, but if you seek the Lord, you 'shall not want' any good thing.

What an assurance, what a promise and what a blessing to know that the Lord is always with us, won't leave us, and if we seek Him, His ways and His plans, we will not want for any good thing.

We won't lack.

The solution to lack, Seek the Lord.

REFLECTION

_____
_____
_____
_____
_____
_____
_____
_____
_____
_____
_____
_____
_____
_____
_____
_____
_____
_____
_____
_____
_____
_____
_____
_____

REFLECTION

_____

_____

_____

_____

_____

_____

_____

_____

_____

_____

_____

_____

_____

_____

_____

_____

_____

_____

_____

_____

_____

_____

_____

SEEK PEACE AND PURSUE IT

"Depart from evil, and do good; **seek** peace, and pursue it."

Psalm 34:14 (KJV)

I can always tell where you're going, what you want, and what you eventually will achieve, by what you do. What you say out of your mouth is important, but normally, that is for your motivation, inspiration and fuel to keep you going. What matters the most is what you are are doing. Whatsoever a man doeth shall prosper. The words mean nothing, but the action means everything.

So, if you talk peace and spend the majority of your time stirring up trouble, trying to find and locating confusion, gossip and every other type of negativity, you don't really want peace. You really enjoy confusion. You enjoy chaos. Now, to have real peace, you have to not only seek it, but the Psalm goes on to say that you have to actually pursue it. Which means that you have to go after it with everything that you have in you. You can talk and apply no effort and expect wonderful things but it won't happen like that. Pursue peace.

Pursuing happens if no one goes, understands or helps you; you are willing to go alone.

Seek peace; don't just talk peace. Pursue it with everything that you've got inside of you.

REFLECTION

REFLECTION

_____

_____
_____
_____
_____
_____
_____
_____
_____
_____
_____
_____
_____
_____
_____
_____
_____
_____
_____
_____
_____
_____
_____
_____
_____

SEEK EARLY

"O God, thou art my God; early will I **seek** thee…"

Psalm 63:1 (KJV)

Seeking God in the morning is not the same as seeking God early. Seeking God early can be viewed in two ways. Early in the morning and/or early in the situation.

I wholeheartedly agree with seeking God in the morning because I am an early riser. I'm normally awake in the dark. But some situations don't happen early in the morning. Some situations, issues, problems or people cause confusion, questions or irritation in the broad daylight or evening. When they rear their ugly heads and spirits, seek God early. Talk to Him about it early. Don't wait hours, days or weeks to speak to Him. Seek out the answer. If fasting and more prayer is necessary, do that too, but most of all, don't wait.

If you're discernment alarm, which is down in your spirit, rises up, waves a red flag or something just does not sit right, ask God about it then.

Seek Him early. It can keep, guard and prevent you from having even more problems, issues and chaos in the future.

Don't wait, seek Him early.

REFLECTION

REFLECTION

_____
_____
_____
_____
_____
_____
_____
_____
_____
_____
_____
_____
_____
_____
_____
_____
_____
_____
_____
_____
_____
_____
_____
_____
_____

SEEK AND LIVE

"The humble shall see this, and be glad: and your heart shall live that **seek** God."

Psalm 69:32 (KJV)

He came that we might have life and we might have that life more abundantly. The best life for us can only be had through God. He really is the only One who knows what's best for us. We should have goals, dreams and desires. We can want things that we are gifted to have and not designed for someone else, but is it really what's best for us?

I admire what other people have, but have been warned that you really don't know what it takes to be that person, get what they have and keep or sustain what they have. As a singer, I wanted to win awards for my music. but the business of music wasn't for me. Now, I win awards for my writing, publishing and books. I have dedicated my life to books and writing, invested more than I ever thought I would and the rewards get me up early in the morning and keeps me up late at night.

So, when I sought God for His plan for my life and said that 'yes', it was worth it. I am in my right mind. I've been disappointed, but I have peace, security and creativeness beyond the hours in a day.

Seek God and live your best life now.

REFLECTION

REFLECTION

_____

_____

_____

_____

_____

_____

_____

_____

_____

_____

_____

_____

_____

_____

_____

_____

_____

_____

_____

_____

_____

_____

_____

_____

_____

_____

_____

_____

SHAMED TO SEEK GOD

"Fill their faces with shame; that they may **seek** thy name, O Lord."

Psalm 83:16 (KJV)

When you go the way that you want to go and not God's path, sometimes He has to get your attention. I recently spoke to a friend who went through a horrific experience with their health. I was prayerful, but I said, "What is God preparing you for, wanting to slow you down for or get you to stop doing?" You don't go through some things for nothing. There is a reason. I'm not saying that the person caused the health issue, but there is a reason for it and it got their attention.

Other times, like this Psalm reminds us, there are those who go through shame in order to seek God. Shame is disappointment and embarrassment. You sometimes have to get embarrassed because you didn't seek or obey God. You have to get rejected, receive a no or 'never' in order to go back, Seek and obey God.

We are all gifted, talented, intelligent, educated and have God-given abilities, but there are some things that are not for us. It may seem like a good thing but it is NOT a God thing.

It's amazing how God is everywhere at the same time but some people only find Him when they are in jail or incarcerated. Some people have to be shamed, get caught and suffer the consequences of their actions before they seek and obey Him.

I don't want to be that person. I want to seek Him, obey Him and enjoy this life until I am no more. Just seek God.

REFLECTION

REFLECTION

_____

_____

_____

_____

_____

_____

_____

_____

_____

_____

_____

_____

_____

_____

_____

_____

_____

_____

_____

_____

_____

_____

_____

_____

The Selfish Seeker

"And **seek**est thou great things for thyself?
seek them not.."

Jeremiah 45:5 (KJV)

There are some people in this world who are
self-centered, which means that they mostly
think about themselves first. There are other
people who are just selfish. These people
rarely take thought of another person. I don't
know how they make good parents, siblings or
co-workers, but they always find who tolerate
their behavior.

Some people feel that they are not selfish, that
they are just preserving their peace, putting up
boundaries or limits. I agree with the
boundaries, but there are some things that are
downright selfish and uncalled for. There are
things you can do that won't cost you money
to help someone else. A smile costs you
nothing. Holding the door open for someone
else costs you in nothing but a few seconds.
No money involved at all.

On the other hand, I'm such a giver that I have
to have someone stop me or I would give
away the world. My parents were givers so it

comes to me naturally. I have to have boundaries, borders, etc. I am learning. Some things, rooms, places, opportunities are NOT meant for everyone. I'm still a work in progress.

Praying selfish prayers. Seeking things just for yourself and not considering others at all should not be done. Sometimes you may be the one who knows, understands and receives great things, but when led and given opportunity, go back and teach the process, the road and the strategy to someone else. Don't seek great things just for yourself; that's a selfish seeker and those selfish things that you seek, you might not receive.

REFLECTION

_____
_____
_____
_____
_____
_____
_____
_____
_____
_____
_____
_____
_____
_____
_____
_____
_____
_____
_____
_____
_____
_____
_____
_____
_____
_____
_____
_____

REFLECTION

_____

_____
_____
_____
_____
_____
_____
_____
_____
_____
_____
_____
_____
_____
_____
_____
_____
_____
_____
_____
_____
_____
_____
_____
_____
_____
_____
_____

SEEK FIRST THE KINGDOM

"But **seek** ye first the kingdom of God, and his righteousness; and all these things shall be added unto you."

Matthew 6:33 (KJV)

God will surpass, go beyond, surprise and overwhelm you with things that you didn't ask for, didn't earn or might not even know that you wanted or needed. He's just that kind of God. I am a living testimony that I'm living a life that I didn't ask for or realize was coming. I was prepared through pain, hardship, disappointment and rejection.

The Word tells us that God will do exceedingly and abundantly above all that we can ask or think according to the power that works in us, but that power comes from Him through obedience and sacrifice. I believed that He could do it, but would He do it for me? Yes. I'm living it. I am seeing Him show up for me each and every day. Allowing me to be in rooms that other people have suggested for me to be in. He has allowed me to meet people online who introduce me to people in my city and state to bless me. Only God can do that. That is exactly what He said would happen when He gave me instructions for my life. He said in the end, "It would be Him and Him alone who would get the credit."

How? I sought Him and followed His plan for my life. It wasn't easy, it wasn't always fun, people didn't understand, and to this day, they still don't understand but to God be the Glory. His Kingdom first will I SEEK.

REFLECTION

REFLECTION

_____

_____

_____

_____

_____

_____

_____

_____

_____

_____

_____

_____

_____

_____

_____

_____

_____

_____

_____

_____

_____

_____

_____

_____

_____

_____

_____

_____

ABOUT THE AUTHOR

Julia Royston spends her days doing what she loves, writing, publishing, speaking about her why and motto, "Helping You Get Your Message to the Masses, Turn Your Words into Wealth and Be a Book Business Boss." Julia is the author of 140+ books, published 400+, recorded 3 music CDs and coached others to be published authors and business owners. She is the owner of five companies, a non-profit organization and the editor of the Book Business Boss Magazine.

To stay connected with Julia, visit www.juliaakroyston.com.

Social Media

Facebook, Instagram, LinkedIN, TikTok and Threads - @juliaaroyston

X - @juliaakroyston

OTHER BOOKS BY JULIA ROYSTON

Julia Royston Books
www.juliaroystonstore.com

Julia Royston Books
www.juliaroystonstore.com

Julia Royston Books
www.roystonchildrenbookstore.com

JOURNAL/SKETCHBOOKS

Julia Royston Books
www.roystonchildrenbookstore.com

Julia Royston Books
www.roystonchildrenbookstore.com

www.ingramcontent.com/pod-product-compliance
Lightning Source LLC
Chambersburg PA
CBHW071948100426
42736CB00042B/2343